Seeing for the First Time

A Child's Unexpected Visions

Billy Jo Collette

Seeing for the First Time

This book, or parts thereof, may not be reproduced in any form without permission. The scanning, uploading and distribution of this book via the Internet or any other means without the permission of the publisher is illegal and punishable by law. Please do not encourage or participate in any form of piracy of copyrighted materials. Your support of the author's rights is appreciated.

ISBN: 978-0-578-45138-1

Book layout/design by:
  Arcand Publishing, *a division of Word Services Unlimited*
  loralee@wordservicesunlimited.com
  wordservicesunlimited.com

Printed in the United States of America.

table of contents

Billy Jo Collette — v
dedicated to Alex Cornelius — vii
introduction — ix

chapter 1 – the start — 1
chapter 2 – the nights — 5
chapter 3 – human helpers — 9
chapter 4 – angels — 15
chapter 5 – the crystal — 21
chapter 6 – heart murmur — 25
chapter 7 – finding Dotti — 31
chapter 8 – power/ strength/ confidence/ growing — 35

a message from my biggest supporter … mom to mom talk — 39
"human helpers" who have inspired me — 42
acknowledgments — 42

Billy Jo Collette

18 years old

Huge enthusiast of mind and body wellness promoted through spiritual communication, Energy Sound Healing, nutrition, and exercise.

Owner and manager of Creating a Healthier You LLC – Energy Sound Healing and healthy living.

Continuing to learn about her spiritual communication gift in classes led by Amy Welinski, Kathi De Baker, and many more…

Offers in-person or long-distance spiritual clearings and learning sessions for crystal children and their parents.

dedicated to Alex Cornelius

I care about and miss you. Thank you for using your presence to allow me to learn and become aware of my gifts as a crystal child.

Mom

Thank you for always listening, understanding me even when "things" didn't always make sense, and for your infinite love and support.

Saradia

You continue to surprise me everyday with your ability to help and protect me throughout challenging times and daily life

introduction

Hi Readers!

As you read my book, you will read some parts which are narrated stories written from memory, and other parts written as "notes" for you to refer back to. This is my journey as I learned and grew as a spiritual communicator. Each and every one of us "crystal children" are different. We are able to connect to the spirits and angels in various ways, whether it be seeing, sensing, hearing, smelling, or feeling.

In each chapter, I share an experience that had a huge impact on my journey thus far. Then at the end I recap the lesson that I believe the universe wanted me to learn and share.

Billy Jo

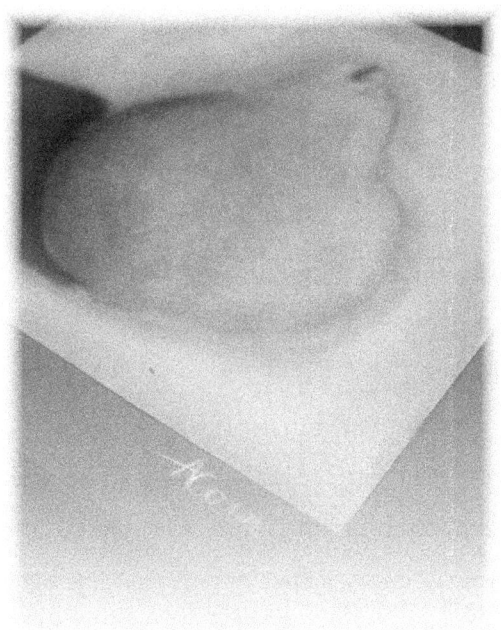

chapter 1
the start

The ambulances, the police cars, the white truck, keys still in the ignition, door swung open, driver not in sight, but motor still running. It was September 2 – the day Alex passed away. The day his lifeless, ice cold-body was found in his bedroom by his mother.

I remember the scene like it was yesterday. Mom, Dad and I peered out our window, not knowing what was going on next door, running about the house in a panic, and unable to concentrate on our normal morning tasks. As Dad loaded my backpack into the back of his truck, I climbed into the

A Child's Unexpected Visions

front seat, both of us trying to carry on with our timely ride to school, despite the obvious distraction only ten feet away.

Dad turned his head, noticing the constant dinging sound coming from the open door of the running white truck parked in our neighbor's driveway alongside the ambulance. He walked across the lawn and turned the key in the ignition, halting the alarming noise. Joining his side, I looked around at the chaos in shock.

Pam, Alex's mother, burst out her front door, frantically trying to light the cigarette that she held in her shaking hand.

"Pam, is everything all right?" Dad asked in a calm but nervous tone. Their eyes met and she shook her head, tears streaming down her face. With a cupped hand, she covered her mouth, large lump in her throat, unable to speak. We waited patiently in disbelief and wonder until she finally muttered the words:

"Alexander killed himself." The words rung in my ears, and both Dad's and my mouths dropped to the ground. Questions raced through my brain: How was it possible that one of my childhood friends whom I had seen just days before was gone? Why did he do this? Had he planned it? What could he possibly have needed to escape from so badly and why did he go to this extent?

My thoughts couldn't steady. I remember Pam and my Dad exchanging a few words, but I was too lost in thought to recall the exact words of reassurance that he had given her. After slowly walking across the lawn, I opened the door to our house with my now-shaking hand, bent over holding my stomach, and crying. Mom rushed over, eyes wide as if searching for answers. I blurted out the exact words that Pam had told Dad and me, as they were still ricocheting inside my skull. "Alexander killed himself."

☙

Sitting in my small sixth grade desk, the day dragged by, my soul and body feeling heavy and lost. But when the final school bell rang and I arrived home, I found my mom sitting on the front steps, eyes glossy, red, and puffy, with a tissue in hand. She stood up as I walked towards her, extending her arms toward me and wrapping me in a big hug. Not much was said by Dad, Mom, or me until dinner time when Mom told us about what she had seen that day. Her vacation day home from work had been spent on our front porch step, watching the police cars and ambulances as they came and went. The most gut-wrenching sight of the day, she said, was watching the hearse being loaded up and pulling away with Alex's body inside, taking him from our neighborhood forever.

As I listened to her talk, the image of Alex's lifeless body being lifted from his bed and being driven away was absolutely terrifying. I broke down as I realized that I would never see him again. Little did I know, that was far from the truth, and I was in for a few more special visits from my childhood friend.

A Child's Unexpected Visions

chapter 2
the nights

A few months after Alex passed, a new nightly ritual started to occur in our household. I was terrified of things I was experiencing, and kept it to myself, believing that if I told anyone, they would think I was crazy.

I saw him. The way he stood, lips pursed, arms crossed, left leg extended slightly to the side, leaning into his right hip, wearing a baggy t-shirt and old fashioned denim jeans. Nothing could deny that it was him, Alex.

His nightly visits to my bedroom doorway left me in complete terror. I tried to protect myself by begging my parents

A Child's Unexpected Visions

to extend their bedtimes, or just altering my own to make sure that one of them was downstairs to "stop" him from climbing the stairs to my bedroom.

My mom had announced to my dad and me that she had a great photography opportunity to travel to another county with some work friends, where she would see some beautiful landscapes and a range of artist eye settings that could really pay off for her photography business. My dad was in full support, but although I knew that she wanted to go, my fear of being left by her, and being unprotected from Alex held me back from feeling the same way. After my tears and the begging, she gave in and decided to stay home. At that point, she knew something was wrong, that something horrible had changed the way I was thinking within the past few months. She needed to know what it was.

Of course I felt terrible for making her stay home, but I didn't know what else to do, much less did I know why my dead friend was appearing in my room every night. After my dad went to bed that night, Mom sat me down on the couch. She asked, "What has happened in this house that is making you so scared?" I burst into tears, and she wrapped me in a hug while wiping my cheeks with the soft paw of my stuffed animal that I had dragged down from my room. I blurted out "Momma, it's Alex." Through the tears, I told her everything and explained that I hadn't told her because I didn't know how she would react. I felt hopeless, out of control, and like I couldn't escape from the fear that I was living in.

Seeing for the First Time

The whole time I was talking, I stared at the floor, but when I finally looked up at her face, she didn't look back. She was staring straight ahead in a trance. I remember thinking to myself, "Oh no, she really does think I'm absolutely crazy." But, moments later, she wrapped me in a tight hug and whispered, "I believe you. We will get through this together. Nothing bad is going to happen." Those words of comfort made me feel as light as a feather, and all the darkness was lifted from my shoulders. I was no longer alone. She was and still is my rock, my shoulder to lean on.

Take away:

Kids: You are not crazy. Don't be afraid to tell your parents. If you need encouragement, remember that I am here as your friend and supporter.

Moms: Listen, believe, and comfort your child. If you notice sudden actions or signs of fear, ask them if everything is OK. This will give them the opportunity to open up to you without having to start the conversation on their own.

A Child's Unexpected Visions

chapter 3
human helpers

Many people have helped and inspired me throughout my journey. I can recall a specific night when my mom was the only person whom I had told about my gift that broadened my view and allowed me to become less closed off to the thought of telling others who could help me learn about my gift.

A few nights after I had told my mom, I couldn't get to sleep. I was tossing and turning, my ears perking up, eyes dashing, and body jolting every time I heard a noise in the house. Crunching my eyelids tightly closed, I begged my angels to help me fall asleep, but it wasn't working. I remember tears soaking my pillow, sweat on my forehead, and the words "Why me" being whispered from my lips. Hearing my mom drawing the sliding kitchen door blinds, clutching the edge of my blankets, and flinging them off my body, I ran down the stairs to the kitchen as fast as I could. My intent being to catch her before she went to bed was complete, but the surprised yet impatient look on her face did not give me any form of comfort.

"I can't fall asleep Momma."

"Billy Jo, I can't keep doing this. It's 11:30 at night."

"I know momma, I know. But I'm scared."

"All right, go upstairs and get to sleep. I'll stay up another half an hour."

"OK," I whimpered before I sprinted back to my bedroom. Throwing myself into bed, my head hit the pillow in just seconds. I was determined that I would beat the "mind game" that night. I failed. As I heard my mom climbing the stairs when the clock struck midnight, I called out her name, but she was too far down the hallway to hear. Rolling to my stomach, face in my pillow, my sprinkling tears turned into a thunderstorm surrounding my cheeks. I was alone. Shifting uncomfortably in my bed, I situated my comforter to stand on end, blocking my bedroom door from view. Face submerged in my childhood, cloud patterned blanket, tears drying on my pale white skin, and body curled into a little ball, I closed my eyes and finally fell asleep.

Seeing for the First Time

When morning came, I woke with my eyes almost swollen shut from last night's tears and was groggy as could be. My mom could tell that I had not slept much that night and wrapped me in a big bear hug and said, "We'll get this fixed, Sweetheart." A grateful slight smile spread across my face, and I hugged her tighter. That day, she scheduled an appointment with a psychic that she had gone to years ago. I remember driving to the appointment on edge, knowing and sensing that Alex had not yet moved on. We walked into the small building, down the long narrow hallway, and to the psychic's office door. The door was open wide and had a long desk parallel to where we were standing. Behind it sat a woman with dark brown, short hair, bright eyes, and a huge smile. I was a bit nervous and uneasy, but during the session her voice was calming as she asked me questions about what I had been experiencing. Because I was unaware that I had the ability to speak with Alex at that time, the woman began speaking to him using her gift and was able to get the message from him. Alex's purpose of visiting me was to give his family closure and free them of any guilt or "what ifs" they were holding on to about his death.

When done explaining, the psychic asked me to close my eyes as she opened the portal that Alex would use to get to heaven. I couldn't believe what I was able to see using my gift as I watched his life like body take a few steps into the tunnel of light. When he reached the top, I saw his face smiling down at me. Leaving that day, I felt great relief because I knew that Alex's spirit was finally at peace.

A Child's Unexpected Visions

I truly believe that everyone and everything comes into our lives at a certain time for a certain reason. Kathi came into my life as the mother of one of my best friends. Her daughter and I were on the same dance team and became very close. Though Olivia and I had been telling stories about each other all year long, our moms finally "met" at our first competition of the season. They had actually been close friends in the past and when seeing each other, they squealed each others names in disbelief.

As the night proceeded, Olivia and I swam in the hotel waterpark for hours, while our moms caught up. It was getting late and the pool started to close down; the extravagant tall rock waterfalls and waterslide flow slowed to a drip and the jungle music clicked off. Olivia and I lugged our weary bodies out of the pool at the call of our mothers' voices, both standing on the overlooking patio balcony.

After saying our goodbyes, I got ready for bed and thought of how nice it was not to be scared of who or what could come into my "field of vision" because my parents were going to be tucked in right beside me. They would protect me from any appearing spirits.

Mom was quieter than usual as she pulled the fresh hotel sheets over my shoulders. She sat down on the edge of my bed, taking my hand in hers, and started to speak.

"Billy Jo, you have a gift, and you're not alone."

I stared back at her, thinking… how do you know?

"Kathi has the gift too sweetie," breathing a sigh of relief as she said it.

Her sigh made me realize that my gift put more stress on her than I could ever had imagined. She hated seeing me scared and secluded. But hearing Kathi's story reassured her that we would make it through the "tough nights and encounters." Mom knew now that she always had a friend to turn to when she couldn't help me on her own.

"Oh," I muttered. I didn't know quite how to respond in the moment. Lying there, I rolled to the other side of the squishy foam hotel mattress and finally processed what my mom had just said. I wasn't alone. Just a few doors down was a woman, Kathi, just like me, and who knew:

"Maybe," I thought to myself, "there were others out there in the world just like us."

Take away:

Kids: There is a whole community of crystal children like us who have this gift, and God gave us this beautiful gift because he knew that we had the heart, passion, and strength to use and help others with it.

Moms: Your kids need all the support from you that you can possibly muster up. Please help them understand how to use their gift and why they have it. Read books or get in contact with spiritual healers in your area. I am here to help too.

A Child's Unexpected Visions

chapter 4
angels

If it weren't for the help of my angels, I don't know how I would have made it thus far in my journey. They have helped me so much throughout my entire life, but it wasn't until I met my angels for the first time that I started to notice their positive impacts. Looking back, I can now recognize significant times in which the angels have shown the power of their abilities. Born at 2 pounds, 6 ounces, through the power of prayer and angels, and of course tons of help from the doctors and the family and friends that surrounded and cared for me, I am here today.

A Child's Unexpected Visions

When I communicate with the universe, I see the infinite number of angels, waiting for people here on earth to ask them for help. At the beginning of my spiritual journey, I had hit bedrock, thinking I was absolutely crazy, but with the help of my angels and the continuous support from my Mom, I have grown and learned more about my gift and what a blessing the power to communicate with the spiritual world really is.

While there can be scary times when demanding spirits make their presence known, I have learned that the angels I have met as well as the ones that fill the universe are always there to help and protect me. Amy Welinski, another one of my "human helpers", a medium, and owner of Golden Light Healing, was the third person that my mom and I went to see to learn more about protecting myself, our family, and our home from the abundance of spirits that were now coming to receive help deciphering their messages and moving their souls on to heaven. She told us that once the spirits know that YOU know you have this gift, flocks of them will come, and boy was she right. They came.

In comfort, one of the first things she asked me was, "You know that you are surrounded by angels, don't you?" I nodded my head. My family has always been churchgoers, so I had heard the Bible stories about angels, but she went on to explain that I had two guardian angels, one to my left and one to my right, that she wanted me to meet that day. She asked me to close my eyes and ask my guardian angels to come forward. To my left is Ashlee, a beautiful feminine character with long, blond hair, and to my right is a handsome masculine angel named Kaleb. Both are always there to protect me. I opened my eyes absolutely stunned at what I had just done. It felt amazing to finally meet my angels and to connect with them using my gift inside my head, rather than seeing them physically like I had seen Alex.

Later that month, Kathi introduced me to an angel named Saradia. Saradia came to Kathi, because at this point in my journey, I was not yet receiving messages from my angels on a regular basis, and she wanted me to know that she was there for me. The moment I met Saradia for the first time, my life changed. She is absolutely extraordinary, as all angels are, but she and I have become extremely close over the years. Saradia is always by my left shoulder, medium length dark brown, spiral curly hair, and a long light pink dress. She is always the one that I turn to when asking for comfort, reassurance, and fun. To show her presence, she leaves heart shaped stones at the beach and presents various heart shaped items for my Mom and I to find in everyday situations.

Archangels have also been a huge part of my life. There are two that I turn to most often: Archangel Michael and Archangel Raphael. When a spirit scares me, I ask Archangel Michael for help. He sends down portals to transport the spirits to heaven. Second, I turn to Archangel Raphael in times of stress or pain. He is an angel that heals the sick and injured, whom I ask to heal myself, family, and friends when they are struggling, as well as any people who correspond with emergency sirens that I hear rushing past throughout the day.

As I said before, there is a whole universe of angels around us; this is how I met the ones that fill my room and home. Around my room, I asked angels to stand in every corner, as well as one at the head, sides, and foot of my bed. My room angels have promised never to leave my side. The house angels are stationed in each compass direction of my home, two to each. When I call upon our family's house angels, I ask them to stay until a certain date. When the date is reached, I ask if they would like to stay and protect our home until the next chosen date, or if they would like to move onto help others. If they do choose to move onto their next adventure or calling, I call in new angels. Together, room and house angels, work hard to help spirits up to heaven rather than letting them roam in my home. They do such an amazing job, and words can't describe how thankful I am to have them in my life.

When meeting these angels, I close my eyes and see the beautiful sky and clouds above that mark the entrance of heaven. Their appearance changes depending on the time of day I communicate. During the night, the universe is lit by infinite stars, while during the daytime, it is lit by beautiful sunbeams peeking through the puffy white clouds. As the angels come forward that would like to help and protect me during this clearing process, I see a golden lit portal form from heaven to my home and the angels gliding through it to introduce themselves. It is incredible.

Seeing for the First Time

Take away:

Kids: Remember that your angels are always there for you no matter what. They will never judge or leave you. It can be fun to look for their "recurring signs" or gifts to you.

Moms: Encourage your children to remember that their angels are always there to protect and help them because fear will sometimes make them forget. If they don't feel comfortable meeting their angels on their own, find someone who can help them.

Both: Look for the recurring signs of an angel's presence. The signs can be physical things that are given to you; for example, like how Saradiya leaves me heart shaped stones but, finding a coin, or feeling something touching your arm, leg, hair, etc. can also be their way of showing you that they are there. Although our schedules can get pretty hectic, try to remember to thank your angels often for their support and presence. Without them, I know that I wouldn't be the positive and ambitious person that I am today. They have helped me through so many obstacles, and I wish to share my story in order to help others know that their angels are there to do the same.

A Child's Unexpected Visions

chapter 5
the crystal

I could sense more and more spirits in my home and was beginning to feel as though I was being taken advantage of. My mom and I couldn't understand why so many were coming all at once. I would cry because their presence would scare me. Though I was beginning to become less anxious when going to sleep, I remember one night in particular that I could not shut my eyes without sensing another spirit next to me. After an hour and a half of trying to fall asleep, I creeped my way downstairs to ask Mom for comfort. She was struggling with the spirits presences herself and could feel the heaviness in the air as well.

A Child's Unexpected Visions

Mom has very strong intuition that has helped her formulate questions for me to ask my angels in situations like this. If there are lots of spirits that are heavy and dark, I don't like to particularly communicate directly with them; so that night I asked Saradiya questions that my mom had told me to. By doing so, we found out that there were nearly 150 spirits in our home and that my angels had let them in because they thought that I was doing something good by helping them move on. Though I was doing something good, the presence of so many spirits was constantly affecting my day-to-day life in a negative way. Helping spirits move on is something that I truly enjoy; however, I knew that I needed to lay down a boundary in order to protect not only myself, but my family as well. I didn't realize it at the time, but having that many spirits and that much energy around me at one time was making me moody, negative, and physically drained.

In addition to setting my boundaries, when going to Amy's, she recommended that we buy a "house crystal", a crystal rock where the spirits go to and stay inside instead of being free to travel around your home that Amy helped us "activate". Now that I have one, when I sense a spirit around me, I calmly ask my angels to take them to the crystal where I will help them to heaven within one or two weeks.

When it is time, my mom and I set aside about 30 minutes of our day to empty the crystal, opening the portals and allowing the spirits to go up to heaven. We have a verse, written by Amy, now memorized in our brains that we say. It reads,

Seeing for the First Time

"We invoke the light from above, below, from the north, south, east and west, and ask that light come strongly to the center of this crystal to help and heal all those souls who are lost. We ask that these souls be provided healing on all levels and for the highest good. We ask that the portals be opened in the directions needed to guide these souls home. Thank you."

You are welcome to use this statement to empty your own crystal if you choose this method of protection for your home, or you can personalize it to create a statement of your own.

Everyone's vision is most likely going to be different when they clear their crystal. For me, I see the outline of the crystal first, then second, I am able to more clearly envision the inside of the crystal. It has glowing, open portals lining the walls, a larger main portal located at the top that leads directly to heaven. Most spirits begin to flow out of the crystal using the portals, but some spirits stand their ground as they don't wish to move on. These are the ones that need a bit more encouragement. To do so, I talk directly to them, their angels, my angels, and the archangels, comforting the spirit to let them know that God will never judge them, as well as asking the angels to help comfort them and move them up to heaven. As they travel up the portal and into heaven, I can see their energy change completely from negative to positive.

After clearing our home, My mom and I can feel that the energy around us is no longer as "heavy". When taking a deep breath in, it feels and smells like the fresh spring air because the spirits have left.

The crystal has helped me grow and learn how to use my gift and better communicate with the spirit world without feeling afraid. War veterans, Las Vegas dancers, children, families, and even ducks and pets have traveled through my crystal. I don't look at any of these spirits as anything less than an actual human here on earth. Each one has their own story and are allowing me to be apart of it, and that is extremely rewarding in itself.

Take away:

Kids: Always remember that it is OK to set your boundaries sternly. Make strong statements to the universe and the spirit world, telling them exactly when you are and are not willing to connect with the other side. For example, I chose to disconnect during the evening, 7pm–8am. At first I did not feel comfortable being so stern with the angels; however, I learned through this experience that if I was not stern about my boundaries, I would be sacrificing my freedom to be present in my "real world" life. Remember that being stern is not the same as being rude.

Moms: If your child is struggling to find the courage to set boundaries, I encourage you to say the words and set the boundaries with them. The universe can hear you even if you don't believe that you have this gift. Also, if spirits are constantly making an appearance in your home, a "house crystal" is something that I would recommend to control their presence.

chapter 6
heart murmur

"Breathe in. Breathe out. Again." I was in for a checkup and was feeling drained and tired. The pediatric doctor took her stethoscope out of her ears and looked at me, then at my mother with a nervous look on her face. She explained that she was hearing a double heartbeat, meaning I had a hole in my heart – a heart murmur. The first words I managed to sputter out of my mouth were, "Will I still be able to dance?"

I glanced at my mom and saw her sorrowed face, eyes fighting back tears.

A Child's Unexpected Visions

"I'm afraid that I'm not able to clear you for any strenuous physical activity," the doctor exclaimed.

I remember pulling my knees up to my chest, feet crinkling the white paper on top of the green foam table, burying my face in my knees, and sobbing. The doctor excused herself at that point, and Mom rushed over and wrapped her arms around me. Minutes later, multiple doctors and nurses barged into the room explaining to my mom that they had to run a few more tests, while hooking up cords and pressing the cold gel pads onto my skin. I was terrified and absolutely devastated. Dance was my passion, my life, and I couldn't imagine a day going by without being in the studio. All tests came back positive. I, in fact, did have a heart murmur. I couldn't dance anymore, and my life was changed.

When my mom and I got home from the doctor, I just laid on the couch, face towards the wall, and closed my eyes. I felt defeated.

I remember peering into the kitchen, seeing my mom sitting at the counter appearing to be doing her computer work, but she was in a dazed state of mind. She spoke in her calm voice, "Billy Jo, what if you don't really have a heart murmur?"

"What do you mean?" I sputtered.

"Well, what if you just have an entity attached to you?"

I stared blankly into my mom's eyes as I came to the realization that this could really be the case. I had known that spirits could attach to your body and had experienced them dragging my energy down doing so; however, I had never imagined that a spirit could affect my health as strongly as this one did.

Mom had Kathi on the phone. Within minutes, she was confirming that yes there was a spirit attached to me, and found out exactly who they were. The spirit's name was Frank. After passing, he regretted some of his decisions as a father. Because of the way he had treated his children, he was afraid of judgment and punishment from God if he tried to enter heaven. Frank chose me to attach to because I was just beginning my journey and was still fearful. My spiritual senses were not terribly strong yet because my fear created a connection block which made him think that I wouldn't be able to sense his presence. After finally hanging up the phone, Mom asked if I was willing to clear this spirit on my own, but I was too afraid to connect with him because he had already caused me so much harm. Kathi did the clearing for me.

Days after the clearing, I had another doctor's appointment scheduled for them to assess my heart condition, a second time with even more tests. The nurse who had treated me just days before took out her stethoscope, listened, and as she did her facial expressions changed. Her jaw just about dropped to the floor. My heart murmur was gone. As she told us this, Mom and I grinned from ear to ear but didn't say a word. The doctors believed it was a miracle. I believe it was just God giving me a challenge to prove my strength and awaken me to what my gift to communicate with the spiritual world really has in store. It

A Child's Unexpected Visions

is so much more than just being able to communicate with my angels and spirits; it is the ability to change how an actual person is feeling, clearing them of negative energy to improve not only their mood but their physical health as well.

Many misconceptions are made when thinking of the spirit world. People tend to believe that the "darker" spirits, like Frank, go to Hell while the good spirits go to Heaven. As Kathi moved Frank on, she was reassuring him that everything would be all right, that God would never judge him. As most religions believe, "God knows everything," which yes, He does. However, they also preach that "there is a Heaven and a Hell." With complete respect for all religions, as I am Christian as well, because of my experiences with this gift, moving spirits on and clearing friends and family of "hitchhikers" and negative energy, I firmly believe that there is not a Hell. "Darker" spirits are just grieving and motivated by fear. For Frank, unfortunately attaching himself to me was the only way of staying on Earth to hide and cope the only way he thought was possible.

Simplicity is one word that I would use to describe Heaven. When helping spirits move on, Heaven appears to be as peaceful and uncomplicated as anyone would believe. In our world, we get caught up in the drama of demanding importance and superiority over others, but in Heaven, none of that exists. Every soul is equal. No one is sent to Hell because of his or her actions, but are rather put into Heaven's positive environment that allows every spirit to worry less, and become the free-feeling soul that they really are. In Heaven, God forgives each spirit like I forgave Frank. Without forgiveness in our world, I wouldn't want to know what it would be like. Even though Frank harmed me, after he went to Heaven and I finally felt comfortable communicating with him, he apologized. I chose to forgive him because his mistake was made out of desperation.

Take aways:

Kids: Be aware of your surroundings and feelings. You will notice a difference in times that spirits are present in your energy field and in times they are not, based on the level of your positivity and overall energy. If you feel comfortable after moving the spirit onto Heaven, make sure that you and your energy field is clear of all negativity that they may have left behind; get to know them a bit. I know it can be scary to connect with spirits, but try asking "Who? What? When? Where? Why? How?" and any other questions you may have for them if you feel comfortable. I personally prefer to communicate with them once they are in Heaven, because I then know that their message is coming from a good place and mindset. Asking questions can help you understand why they came to you. Though some people may have persuasive beliefs on equality, I encourage you to find your own viewpoint. Allow that viewpoint to factor into your lifestyle instead of going along with what others tell you to believe.

Moms: If you notice a difference in your child's actions, energy level, or personality, ask them if they will sit down with

A Child's Unexpected Visions

you to make sure that there are no spirits attached to them or their energy field that are dragging them down. Having my mom by my side coming up with the right questions to ask and supporting me comforted me enough to be able to communicate with the spirit when I was scared. Never doubt your ability to formulate questions, even if you don't believe you have great intuition to help you ask the right questions. Start with asking the basic "Who? What? When? Where? Why? How?" questions, then grow into detail from there.

chapter 7
finding Dotti

The last experience that I would like to share is quite an extraordinary one. To jump right in, this particular winter had been a brutal one in Wisconsin. Laurie, a work colleague of my mom's, came to her one day and said, "I'm not sure why I'm telling you this, but I just feel like I need to. My neighbors have a little cat that got outside and took off. It's cold, and she got so scared when they tried to chase her. Now she's hiding and they can't find her. Is there a way that you can help?"

A Child's Unexpected Visions

Laurie had limited knowledge of my ability to communicate, so my mom filled her in a little bit and said she would talk to me and see what we could do.

At dinner that night, mom explained the situation and asked if I thought I could help. I was almost in tears thinking about Dotti being lost out in the below zero degree weather, and of course said I would try. I settled into my room and began by surrounding the kitty with three "bubbles" — a white bubble for protection, a purple bubble for healing, and a pink bubble for love. Archangels Michael and Rafael came in when I called, as well as additional help from my angels and Dotti's own angels, to keep her warm and healthy until she was found.

Step two was to ask my angels where Dotti was. The image of a flat wooden back porch appeared in my mind. Details came into vision. It was lifted six inches off the ground with no sides attached. The next day, I called my mom at work and described the house that the porch was attached to. Mom drew a picture as I described it, a story-and-a-half house with the garage to the right, a lot of bushes, and the porch off the back. She showed the picture to Laurie, and they pulled the house up on the internet. Across the street from Dottie's real home was a vacant house that looked exactly like the picture I described. Laurie put her coat on and left work immediately to go look. Mom and I went over to the house after she had gotten home from work and looked around the yard for about 20 minutes with no luck, but we kept asking the angels to help guide Dotti home.

Seeing for the First Time

The next evening, Mom was sorting through a few papers in her office and found two pictures that I had drawn her when I was little. One was a drawing of a cat crossing the street, and another was of an angel with the words "I am an angel, I am here to help you" written across her dress. Upon finding these, she called me downstairs from my bedroom, handed them to me, and said, "There's no space or time."

After looking but not finding the cat the night before, I was feeling a bit discouraged, but her finding the pictures and understanding the universe's message to keep trying gave me all new motivation to find Dotti no matter how much energy and time I needed to put in to complete my readings. Lying in bed that night, I asked Saradia to show me where Dotti was. As I did, I saw an image of a porch, much like the one I had seen before, yet smaller, higher up, and attached to a home that was being lived in. I told mom, "Dottie is under another porch now. I think it is her own home. She is going back and forth between the houses." It was too late at night to text Laurie, but Mom told her the next day.

The following day after Mom shared this news, Laurie came into work and said, "Dottie is home! She was hiding under her own porch, and when they would try to get her out, she would scoot out of reach. Finally they took a board off and just reached in and grabbed her."

All of my information had been correct! The Angels helped me find her, Dottie was home!

A Child's Unexpected Visions

Whenever I think about this instance and the heartwarming feeling that I had when Dotti was found, a huge smile spreads across my face. This being the last experience that I share with you in this book, my interpretation of its message wraps up what I want you to take away if nothing else.

Take aways:

Kids: First off, your gift is real; don't doubt it or yourself. You wouldn't be reading this book if you didn't have some sort of reason to believe that you have this gift. Second, trust your intuition and look for the signs that the universe is trying to show you. Third, there is no space or time in the spirit and angel world, so everything happens for a reason. Fourth, be the leader that you are; stay determined, motivated and true to yourself, focus on your goals, and reach for your dreams. You will get through the tough and scary times and will grow into the amazing individual that I believe in and know you are.

Moms: I've been preaching it throughout every chapter, but please, please, please listen, believe, and support your child through every step of their journey as they learn and grow. They need YOU.

chapter 8
power/ strength/ confidence/ growing

While every spiritual journey has a starting point, it will never have an ending point; this gift is yours forever. You are born with it, but your first noticeable experiences will not occur until the universe knows you are ready and able to handle the responsibilities that come with it. By experiencing the things that I have written about, I have grown as a person because I have learned to decipher and understand each lesson that the universe was trying to teach me. Not only does my journey enclose strictly the experiences that I have talked about in this book, but also life changing ones that are very near and dear to my heart; such as, the angels helping me calm my nerves before performing at dance competitions and their continuous support throughout my years as a teen. I know that my angels are always looking out for me without me even having to ask.

Because children like us are so sensitive to the energy around us, try your best to surround yourself with people who support you, who are caring, and kind as much as possible. In times when the people you surround yourself with are not in your control, remember that a white protection bubble will do the trick of blocking out any negativity brought on by others. You are a strong and special child. God gave you this gift not to scare you, but because it is real, and because he knew YOU, of all people, could handle it. I know it can be scary, but I promise that you will make it through those times. When you show your fear or anger to the darker spirits that visit, they begin to feel power over you. Don't let them feel as though they have control over you, stand your ground, help them on to heaven, but do so on your terms.

When I'm scared, I have a ritual that I calmly go through to protect myself and move the spirit on.

1. Ask your angels and the universe to allow you to create a strong white protection bubble around yourself.
2. Ask Archangel Michael to send down a strong portal that can be a transfer tunnel for the spirit into heaven.

3. Comfort the spirit while they are moving on either on your own or by asking your angels for help to do so as well, until you know that the spirit has made it to Heaven.
4. Tell Archangel Michael that the spirit is in heaven now and that he can close the portal.
5. Ask your angels to remove any negative energy that the spirit may have left behind from your body, energy field, or environment around you and give it back to Mother Earth. I like to say the Lord's Prayer while they do so.
6. Thank your angels for their help.

I will always be here to be your "human helper".

Moms: My message to you may be simple, but BELIEVE YOUR CHILDREN. Their gift is real. Comfort them and tell them that everything is going to be all right. Speaking from experience, there is nothing more nerve wracking than getting up enough courage to tell your parents about having a spiritual experience for the first time. I would have been devastated and even more terrified than I already was if my mom had not believed and comforted me.

Because your crystal child has this gift, the spirits will continue coming to them because they don't know how to move on, but recognize that your child has the ability to communicate and help them. Without my mom's help, I would have continued to believe that I was crazy and never would have learned how to get control over their presence.

A Child's Unexpected Visions

Please listen to your child. I understand that it may be hard to grasp at first and may seem a bit scary, but think about how uneasy you are then compare it to how your child must be feeling. THEY NEED YOU.

To all my readers:

I consider you all part of my family, care about each and every one of you, and wish you all nothing but the best in your futures. Everyone has their own journey with different experiences. We all live different lives, but together, our community of crystal children have the ability to touch the lives of millions. Together, we help each other through the tough times and celebrate the happy ones by helping one spirit move on at a time.

Now, a message from my biggest supporter...

mom to mom talk

Moms (Parents),

The only thing that prepared me to give the response my daughter needed when she gasped and sobbed the words, "Momma! It's Alex..." was Love itself.

I didn't know a lot about the "Spirit World" at the time, but I did know my daughter. The sudden change in her behavior that was taking place in our home at bedtime was not normal behavior. The last two months of asking me to stay up, asking if she could sleep in our room, asking if I would sleep in her room, sometimes pleading often near tears — it all made perfect sense when the words tumbled from her mouth.

It was my unquestionable responsibility as her mother to find out as much as I could about what she was seeing, why she was seeing, and what we were supposed to do about it.

The journey began in that moment, the first step, listening to what she had to say.

Using her information, I was able to ask questions, make phone calls, read books, attend workshops, and learn, for both of us, so we could understand and protect ourselves from this very real other world.

A Child's Unexpected Visions

We were fortunate to seek out the help of two very trusted sources: Amy Wilinski of Golden Light Healing and Kathi DeBaker of Inspired to Heal.

In my first call to Amy, she said, "Honey, you need to learn how to put boundaries around yourselves and your home. Spirits that are 'stuck' know who can see, and they will come." Seriously? What? You've got to be kidding me.... How do you even process this information? You "listen to your child" and help your child navigate through what they are seeing. In our case, Billy Jo would communicate while I would help her navigate and figure out what to do next.

Both Amy and Kathi immediately turned us to our angels. Sure we all have angels. We learned that in church, right? Well, we have angels like you can't believe, and my daughter can talk to them like they are sitting right next to you (they are).

It is with their help that we have been able to learn, manage, protect, and help others.

Listen to your child. The information that flows freely is nothing they can make up. The names, the descriptions, the stories...Not the normal dialogue from a child.

Billy Jo has become very strong with "her gift". She has been able to help many lost souls / spirits to move on. As she begins to let other people know about her gift, she has been able to help other children and adults understand the things that they are seeing and witnessing in their lives.

Seeing for the First Time

My daughter is making a difference. She is not sick, crazy, or irrational. She has a gift. As her mother, I loved her, trusted her and helped her learn how to manage it.

Moms and parents, embrace and listen. Your child is not crazy because what they see and experience is unfamiliar to you. Help them grow. Love them, trust them, and listen to them.

And to My Sweet Girl, thank you for trusting me enough to tell me the truth so we could work this out together. I couldn't be more proud of your courage, your compassion, and your love for life.

"Continue to be amazing."

Love, Mom

A Child's Unexpected Visions

"human helpers" who have inspired me

Mary Collette — My mom
   Owner of Mary's Canvas LLC – Artist
   Co-Owner of Inspire Gallery

Amy Wilinski
   Owner of Golden Light Healing – Medium

Kathi De Baker
   Owner of Inspire to Heal – Medium/ Reiki Master
   Co-Owner of Inspire Gallery

acknowledgments

chapter 1 artwork
   The illustration of the pear was drawn by Alex Cornelius. He signed it with his nickname … "Acorn".

chapter photos
   The images on each chapter first page were photographed by my mom, Mary Collette.

A Child's Unexpected Visions

www.ingramcontent.com/pod-product-compliance
Lightning Source LLC
Chambersburg PA
CBHW061259040426
42444CB00010B/2425